Shaping Up Summer

written by

Lizann Flatt

illustrated by

Ashley Barron

Owl
kids

Do you think that math matters to the animals and plants?

What if nature knew numbers like you?

Let's look at summer.

Imagine what shapes and a sense of space could do!

If you were near,
this fact would appear:
the Sun is actually
the shape of a sphere.

Most of these pairs of lines are parallel.
Can you find the ones that aren't?

Sunlight travels away from the Sun,
and all the Earth soaks it in.
Imagine seeing these warm lines of light
giving color to feathers and warming up skin.

Might the moles mine in shapes,
digging doodles in the dirt?

Can you see a square, a circle,
a triangle, and a rectangle?
What other shapes do you see?

Would spiders weave webs
to spin silken scenes?

What shapes do you see in the pictures on
the spider web? Can you find all the squares?

Should skunks sketch warning shapes onto the ground before turning their black-and-white backsides around?

Which skunk has made only triangles? What shape rules are the other skunks following?

Could the crabs excavate,
then take time to decorate
their doorways with shapes of sand?

Can you see a sphere, a cube, a rectangular prism, a pyramid, and a cylinder?

Would the narwhals sort the ice?
Choose the chunks they think are nice?

Can you see cone shapes? Which ice chunk shapes have circle faces? Square faces?

Maybe beavers would build dams
following fancy people plans?

How many three-dimensional shapes can
you see here? Do you see a shape with
1 face? 2 faces? 3 faces? More faces?

Since puffins stay put in the same summer spaces,
would they memorize directions to find their own places?

Which word or phrase describes each puffin's location in relation to
its burrow: inside, outside, in front of, behind, between, or beside?

Would insects know
if their flight paths go
over or under,
above or below?

Which insect flew over, under, above, or below something?
Follow the dotted lines to find out.

When dolphins dip or dolphins dive,
do they decide to turn, flip, or slide?

Comparing the left and the right scenes, can you describe how each dolphin has moved?

Could coyotes keep track
of where the cool spots are at?
Do you think they would map
secret places to nap?

**Using the legend, can you find the
closest place for each of these coyotes
to stay cool and hide during the day?**

COYOTE HIDING PLACES

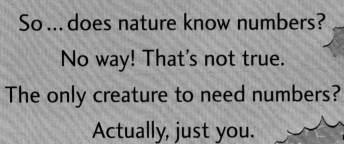

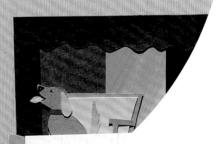

So ... does nature know numbers?
No way! That's not true.
The only creature to need numbers?
Actually, just you.

How is the child in the center keeping cool? How are the kids keeping cool in the upper left? The middle right?

Nature Notes

In the summer, female alligators build nests of grasses and lay about 30 eggs. Alligators are cold-blooded, which means they have to sit in the sun to warm up. Painted bunting males are colorful birds. Some of their vibrant colors, especially blue and shiny metallic, are made when sunlight hits their specially structured feathers.

Moles dig tunnels in the dirt at all times of the day or night and hardly ever appear above ground. Some tunnels are for traveling, and some are for finding food. Deeper tunnels are for nests and to escape summer heat or winter cold. Moles get rid of the dirt from a tunnel by pushing it up to the surface, making mounds we call molehills.

Orb weaver spiders spin large circular webs to trap insects. The webs have sticky threads for capturing the insect and non-sticky threads for the spider to walk on. These spiders bite a trapped insect and wrap it in silk before eating it. Spider webs are most noticeable in late summer when the spiders have grown to full adult size and spin larger webs.

In the summer, female skunks take their babies out at night to teach them how to find insects, berries, worms, and beetles. If they are threatened, they will give warning signs by growling, hissing, or stamping their feet on the ground. If the danger doesn't leave, the skunk will turn its backside and spray a smelly mist.

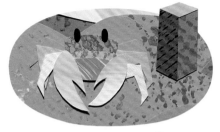

Adult **ghost crabs** live on warm, sandy ocean beaches. Some ghost crabs dig holes in the sand with their large claws and pile the sand just outside the holes in neat cone-shaped mounds. Others push the sand out, scattering it in a fan shape. They spend the day in the cool, moist hole and search for food at night.

In the Arctic summer, **narwhals** move to feeding grounds where the solid ice has melted, leaving broken chunks of ice and icebergs. Baby narwhals are born in July and August. The cone-shaped tusk, which is a long tooth, grows only on males. Narwhals eat cod and squid, but they don't eat as much in summer as in fall or winter.

Beaver kits first come out of their lodge in the summer. They stay with their parents and older brothers or sisters for about two years. Beavers eat water lilies, cattails, leaves, twigs, grasses, fruit, and herbs in summer. They repair and maintain the lodge and dam with sticks and mud. In late summer, beavers save twigs in piles underwater so they'll have winter food nearby.

Puffins usually return to the same burrow with the same mate every year. They dig their burrows in grassy ocean cliff sides, cracks under boulders, or rock crevices. Adults swim under water to catch small fish to bring back to their single chick. The chick grows all summer until it has feathers, and then it jumps into the ocean and swims away!

Dog-day or annual cicadas live for only five to six weeks and do not usually fly far from trees. Hummingbird moths hover close to flowers and sip nectar with their long, thin proboscises. Grasshoppers eat plants and have strong back legs to help them hop. They can also fly. Bumblebees gather pollen and nectar from all different kinds of flowers.

Eastern newt larvae hatch out of eggs under water. They eat and grow all summer, then transform into the red eft stage and spend two to three years on land. They then transform into aquatic adults and return to live in slow-moving waters. They have poisons in their skin to protect them from predators. They can live for 10 years.

Dolphins live in groups in warm ocean waters. They love to chase one another, throw seaweed around, and ride the waves made by boats. They jump out of the water and land on their backs, sides, or bellies. A dolphin breathes air from a hole in the top of its head. It can dive for about 10 minutes.

Coyotes are found in almost every major city in North America, living in parks, ravines, abandoned lots, and back alleys. In summer, adults hunt for mice, rabbits, and squirrels. But coyotes will also eat garbage, birdseed, and fruit fallen from trees. They mostly travel at dawn and dusk, but they can be seen at any time of the day.

To Paul, for shaping a fantastic family—the foundation for my writing. Thank you!
~Lizann

To Claudia, Jennifer, Mahak, and Barb, for making this series the best it could possibly be.
~Ashley

The author wishes to acknowledge the support of the Ontario Arts Council through the Writers' Reserve program.

Owlkids Books acknowledges the financial support of the Canada Council for the Arts, the Ontario Arts Council, the Government of Canada through the Canada Book Fund (CBF) and the Government of Ontario through the Ontario Creates Book Initiative for our publishing activities.

Published in Canada by
Owlkids Books Inc.
1 Eglinton Avenue East
Toronto, ON M4P 3A1

Published in the United States by
Owlkids Books Inc.
1700 Fourth Street
Berkeley, CA 94710

Library and Archives Canada Cataloguing in Publication

Flatt, Lizann, author
    Shaping up summer / written by Lizann Flatt ; illustrated by Ashley Barron.

(Math in nature ; 4)
ISBN 978-1-926973-87-6 (bound).--ISBN 978-1-77147-163-3 (softcover)

    1. Shapes--Juvenile literature. 2. Geometry in nature--Juvenile literature. 3. Summer--Juvenile literature.
I. Barron, Ashley, illustrator II. Title. III. Series: Flatt, Lizann. Math in nature ; 4

QA445.5.F53 2014   j516'.15   C2013-904157-5

Library of Congress Control Number: 2017952470

Design: Claudia Dávila

ONTARIO ARTS COUNCIL
CONSEIL DES ARTS DE L'ONTARIO
an Ontario government agency
un organisme du gouvernement de l'Ontario

Canada Council
for the Arts
Conseil des Arts
du Canada

Canadä

Manufactured in Shenzhen, China, in April 2022, by C&C Joint Printing Co.
Job #HW1716

D   E   F   G   H   I

FSC
MIX
Paper from responsible sources
FSC® C008047

Publisher of Chirp, Chickadee and OWL
www.owlkidsbooks.com

Owlkids Books is a division of bayard canada